# MIAMI AIRPORT

# MIAMI AIRPORT

## John K. Morton

**Airlife**
England

# Dedication

This book is dedicated to my wife Margaret, in appreciation of her encouragement and support, and for her patience and understanding whilst I have spent many hours in and around the airport during our many trips to Miami.

First published in the UK in 1999
by Airlife Publishing Ltd

**British Library Cataloguing-in-Publication Data**
A catalogue record for this book
is available from the British Library

ISBN 1 84037 061 0

Typeset by Rowland Phototypesetting Ltd,
Bury St Edmunds, Suffolk.
Printed in Hong Kong.

**Airlife Publishing Ltd**
101 Longden Road, Shrewsbury, SY3 9EB, England
E-mail: airlife@airlifebooks.com
Website: www.airlifebooks.com

# Introduction

Since its development in 1928, Miami International Airport (MIA) has become one of the most dynamic airports in the world's arena of transportation. As the number one international cargo and number two passenger airport in the United States, Miami International Airport is maintaining its leadership with innovative approaches to cargo and passenger services.

As the gateway to Latin America, a market totalling in excess of 300 million consumers, Miami International Airport is the transit hub for international passengers and air cargo between Latin America and the world. The airport is served by more airlines than any other airport in the western hemisphere with almost 100 scheduled and 40 charter companies averaging 1,500 flights per day with services from 200 cities on five continents, including more flights from Latin America than all other US airports combined.

Each month, more than one million international passengers transit MIA and this figure is estimated to rise by 115% by the year 2010. In a recent study by the FAA, it was estimated that it is the nation's fastest-growing airport and that by the year 2010 flight operations, take-offs and landings, will rise to 930,000 per year. The existing airfield facilities are fast approaching maximum capacity and in order to avoid unacceptable and costly delays, the proposed fourth runway is needed to alleviate the current congestion. This new runway will be 8,600 feet in length and located north of the existing 9L/27R runway. It will be used primarily for arriving traffic and will be capable of handling the largest commercial airliners.

Miami International Airport covers an area of 3,230 acres and employs a workforce of 40,000 people. Situated within the terminal is a DeLuxe hotel with 230 guest rooms. Three runways are currently in use: 9L/27R which is 10,500 feet in length; 9R/27L which is 13,000 feet long; and cross runway 12/30 which is 9,355 feet in length.

Freight traffic at MIA reached an all-time high of 1.5 million tons of international freight for the 12-month period ending 30 April 1997, a figure that is projected to increase to 2 million tons. Miami International Airport surpassed Tokyo Narita in 1996 to become the second busiest airport in the world for total freight, and is the leader in trade between the United States, Latin America and the Caribbean in both weight and value of cargo.

Cargo City is situated in the south-west corner of MIA between runways 12 and 9R, and when new construction is completed almost 3 million square feet of cargo handling space will be available at the airport. FedEx (Federal Express) are due to open a new $50 million facility at MIA in 1999 which will strengthen the carrier's global express network. The 31-acre site will contain a new 180,000 feet facility with dedicated parking for up to 11 wide-body aircraft.

# Author's Note

Miami International Airport is a further title in the airport series of books published by Airlife and I am honoured to be given the opportunity to produce this volume. I have visited Miami 22 times since my first trip from the United Kingdom in 1978 and have been fortunate to record the MIA scene on film on each occasion.

This volume intends to illustrate Miami International Airport through the 1990s and all pictures reproduced within the pages are from my collection taken during this period. In obtaining some of these photographs I am much indebted to my very good friends Hernando Vergara and Nelson V. Paganacci of Metro-Dade Aviation Department Public Affairs Office for their help and patience. I am also pleased to acknowledge their authorised use of extracts from official publications, and the use of their official 'bird's eye view' photograph of MIA reproduced on the back cover. My thanks go to all Metro-Dade personnel who assisted me in their official capacities.

John K. Morton

BELOW: When warehouses are not available for the loading and unloading of freight, certain ramp areas located near NW36 Street are made available for that purpose. McDonnell Douglas DC-8 N803MG receives the attention of the ground crew whilst waiting to receive pallets of freight. In this December 1995 photograph, the DC-8 carries Trans Continental titles, applied whilst on lease from American International Airways, of which the carrier is a subsidiary.

LEFT: Miami International Airport is also called Wilcox Field and the title is proudly displayed above the central entrance to the terminal building. This entrance also leads to the DeLuxe Hotel situated within the terminal, and guests may travel from the upper floors of the property to a roof-top pool and bar via the glass enclosed elevator.

WILCOX FIELD

MIAMI INTERNATIONAL AIRPORT

APA  AIR JAMAICA  LTU  MIAMI AIR  HOTEL  BALAIR/CTA  FINNAIR  KIWI  AEROMAR  SUN COUNTRY

Located at several prominent positions around the terminal are illuminated signs displaying the layout of the airport.

There are currently eight concourses within the terminal, each identified by the letters 'A' to 'H'. To enable intending passengers to locate their check-in area, the names of airlines operating from each concourse are displayed in appropriate positions on the canopy running along the whole length of the terminal.

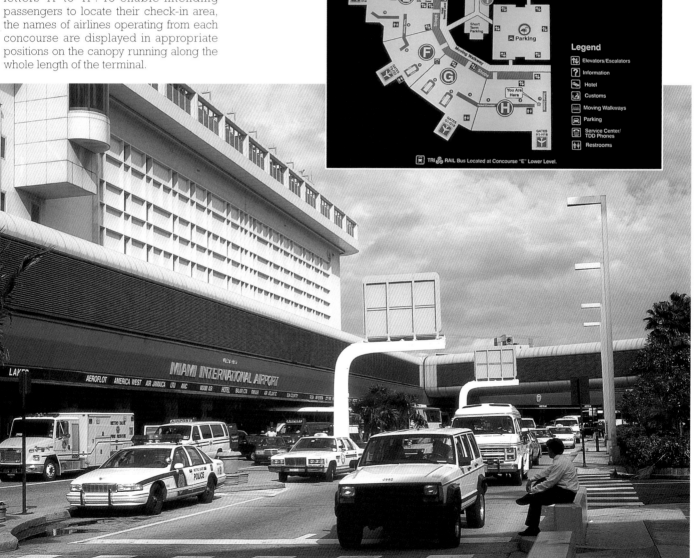

ABOVE: The lower driveway around MIA Terminal is for arriving passengers, baggage claim, car rental counters and Customs, plus ground transportation services, whilst the upper driveway is reserved for departing passengers. The latter driveway can become very congested at busy periods as cars and buses attempt to discharge intending passengers.

Flight departure information is displayed on TV screens within each of the eight concourses, providing details of services departing from gates situated within.

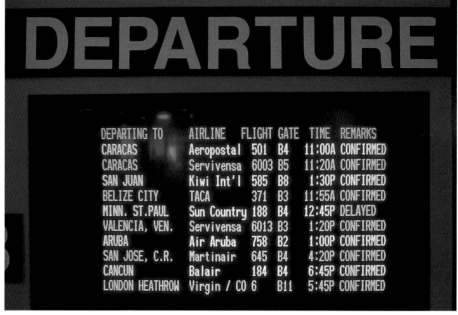

| DEPARTING TO | AIRLINE | FLIGHT | GATE | TIME | REMARKS |
|---|---|---|---|---|---|
| CARACAS | Aeropostal | 501 | B4 | 11:00A | CONFIRMED |
| CARACAS | Servivensa | 6003 | B5 | 11:20A | CONFIRMED |
| SAN JUAN | Kiwi Int'l | 585 | B8 | 1:30P | CONFIRMED |
| BELIZE CITY | TACA | 371 | B3 | 11:55A | CONFIRMED |
| MINN. ST.PAUL | Sun Country | 188 | B4 | 12:45P | DELAYED |
| VALENCIA, VEN. | Servivensa | 6013 | B3 | 1:20P | CONFIRMED |
| ARUBA | Air Aruba | 758 | B2 | 1:00P | CONFIRMED |
| SAN JOSE, C.R. | Martinair | 645 | B4 | 4:20P | CONFIRMED |
| CANCUN | Balair | 184 | B4 | 6:45P | CONFIRMED |
| LONDON HEATHROW | Virgin / CO | 6 | B11 | 5:45P | CONFIRMED |

Each airline operating from Miami has check-in desks and areas devoted for their own use. Passengers for Tower Air's New York service have already arrived and are waiting to check-in.

Located at the entrance to concourse B gates is one of many refreshment areas available to airport users. The modern appearance of this cocktail bar certainly looks welcoming. Signs throughout the terminal are displayed both in Spanish and English.

Previously operating as four separate airlines, Aviateca, Lacsa, Nica and Taca have combined their services and now operate under the 'Grupo Taca' name. Two passengers are being helped with their travel plans.

In common with most large international airports, Miami's terminals are constantly crowded. However, the layout of the check-in areas ensures that wherever possible an uninterrupted flow of passengers is maintained. All check-in desks are located on one side of the terminal, whilst retail outlets are situated on the other.

Small rest areas where passengers may relax with a coffee and bagel prior to joining their flight are positioned within the terminal.

ABOVE: On the north side of Miami International Airport can be seen a number of hangars where repairs and conversions are carried out. The length of time an airliner is present in any facility can vary enormously from an overnight engine change, to a matter of months in cases where an airliner is completely modified and repainted. In this photograph, taken in December 1997 at the PMS facility, a variety of aircraft are undergoing attention.

Departing international passengers are provided with facilities to purchase duty-free goods from several conveniently placed outlets. These are to be found both landside and airside.

Air Jamaica fly regularly into and out of Miami and here passengers are being processed for one of the carrier's daily flights. The Air Jamaica staff have made a special effort to give their passengers a holiday feeling with Christmas displays adorning the desks.

LEFT AND BELOW: Miami Air International is a privately owned charter airline and was established in August 1990. Its headquarters are situated on NW36 Street and from its Miami main hub, a fleet of seven Boeing 727s provides services to the Caribbean, North, Central and South America. N804EA is an ex-Eastern Airlines aircraft and was photographed on the Miami ramp in April 1992 between duties. This airliner was one of the first in the fleet to carry the Miami Air colours and carries the name *Lois*.

OPPOSITE ABOVE: The PMS facility was involved in preparing Boeing 727s for the re-launch of Laker Airways in 1992. This carrier re-started services from a base in the Bahamas with three examples of the type leased from the North American airline USAir. In April 1992, N743US was being prepared to commence flying for Laker. The original USAir colours were retained and the outline of the Laker titles can be seen, having recently been applied to the sides of the fuselage to be filled in later.

OPPOSITE BELOW: McDonnell Douglas DC-8 N819SL, photographed in April 1992 in the colours of Hispaniola Airways, had returned to Miami for attention from the engineers. This 1966-built airliner flew in these colours for a period of sixteen months following earlier service with Antares Airlines.

ABOVE: Services from Miami to the Caribbean Islands are now operated by Beechcraft and Dash 7 aircraft, although Shorts 360s have also been utilised in the past. Regular flights operate in both directions serving Freeport, Governor's Harbour and Nassau. Gulfstream International Airlines is based in Miami and has served the region since its formation in 1990. Its present fleet consists entirely of Beechcraft 1900 nineteen-seat twin-engined aircraft, although in December 1996 the airline was flying Shorts 360s. Photographed at that time was one of the fleet, N262GA, which flew carrying additional stickers promoting the Sandals Resort.

ABOVE: The head of Paradise Island Airlines at the time this picture was taken in January 1990 was the TV show presenter Merv Griffin. This Fort Lauderdale-based airline flies between Nassau and the US mainland and the colour scheme applied to Dash 7 N780MG has now been superseded by that shown in the photograph appearing at the foot of page 52.

BELOW: In January 1998, Pan Am Airbus A300s had already been taken out of service following the earlier re-launch of this world famous airline in 1996. A small fleet of six of the type was put into service on the carrier's new east–west coast routes, but following the termination of these flights due to low passenger figures, the aircraft became surplus to requirements. Two A300s still in the Pan Am livery were photographed receiving attention for possible future use by alternative carriers.

RIGHT: Heavy repairs are carried out at several facilities and Staf Cargo's McDonnell Douglas DC-10 XA-TDC is receiving attention to its tail-mounted engine. Staf is a Buenos Aires-based airline and regularly flies from Argentina to Miami. The aircraft returned to service shortly after this photograph was taken in January 1998.

OPPOSITE ABOVE: After the unfortunate third failure of Braniff International Airlines, its fleet of Boeing 727s was parked at various locations around the States awaiting a possible purchaser. The third attempt by the airline to take to the air began in December 1990 with services continuing until summer 1992. Boeing 727 N8856E was one of eight airliners taken out of service and stored upon the cessation of flights, being photographed in December 1996, minus an engine and still awaiting a buyer.

OPPOSITE BELOW: Areas in the north-east corner of the airport are reserved for parking aircraft between duties. In this December 1995 photograph, Boeing 747 N4724UA of United Airlines had arrived at the passenger terminal earlier that morning and was towed to this location until the scheduled time to be returned to the terminal for an overnight flight. This procedure allows the airport authority to make full use of available gates.

OPPOSITE ABOVE: Boeing 727 HC-BIB was photographed in December 1995 in the parking area of the airport, although not between duties at the time. The port fuselage-mounted engine had been removed for attention although no other servicing work is apparent. SAN – Servicios Aereos Nacionales – is a Guayaquil, Ecuador-based passenger airline and this aircraft has carried its company colours since 1981.

OPPOSITE BELOW: The Brazilian airline VARIG operates a daily non-stop service from Rio de Janeiro, a flight performed by one of the carrier's Boeing 747 series 300 aircraft at the time this photograph was taken in January 1998. The overnight flight from the Brazilian city arrives around 05.30hrs, and as the return service is not scheduled to depart until almost midnight the aircraft is parked for most of the day. PP-VNH is seen surrounded by baggage containers at the eastern end of the airport, the newly acquired livery catching the last rays of the evening sun.

BELOW: The Florida East Coast Railroad track runs parallel to the airport perimeter road on the south side, and carries around three or four freight trains daily. Most of the trains are in excess of 90 vehicles, taking five or six minutes to pass. Flying over this passing freight train in January 1990 is an Eastern Airlines McDonnell Douglas DC-9 which will land on runway 30, no doubt reaching its gate before the last vehicle of the train passes the photographer.

BELOW: Airbus A310 HC-BRB, wearing the flamboyant colours of Ecuatoriana, has already released brakes and has commenced its take-off roll along runway 12. This Ecuador-based South American airline has been flying into and out of Miami for many years. When photographed in January 1993, two A310s were operating to Miami in this colour scheme, but all services were suspended in September of that year. It was the company's intention to restart during the following months, and services did in fact recommence in early 1996, with Miami again being one of the carrier's major destinations.

OPPOSITE ABOVE: Rich International Airways was formed in 1970 as a scheduled and charter operator flying from its Miami base. The airline had its own facility situated alongside NW36 Street where aircraft in the company fleet could be seen and photographed. In April 1992, Lockheed L1011 N303EA was photographed whilst being prepared to operate a charter flight to South America. The aircraft was originally flown by Eastern Airlines and still bears the registration assigned to that carrier, entering service with Rich in May 1991. Rich International continued to provide flights with its fleet of McDonnell Douglas DC-8s and Lockheed L1011s until suspending operations in 1997.

OPPOSITE BELOW: Additional FAA-approved repair stations are located west of NW57 Avenue with large ramps to accommodate aircraft awaiting servicing and those recently completed. In this December 1992 shot, McDonnell Douglas DC-10 N602DC is being worked on outdoors. Lineas Aereas Paraguayas was formed in 1963 with a base in Asunción. The airline suspended operations in March 1994 and at that time this DC-10 was the only wide-body airliner in the carrier's fleet of six aircraft.

BELOW: Runway 9L is being used for the landing of Renown Aviation's Electra N356Q in January 1996. This California-based regional and domestic cargo carrier currently performs operations with a fleet of Convairs and Lockheed Electras.

OPPOSITE ABOVE: *Miami Heat* is the name given to the city's basketball team and is seen here applied to Boeing 727 N8866E. The aircraft was part of the Carnival Airlines fleet and fitted with 30 first-class seats, and utilised to transport the team and staff to away games. The 727 replaces a Boeing 737 which provided a similar service and carried identical colours. Photographed in January 1996, the tri-jet awaits its next flight.

OPPOSITE BELOW: Airliners used by basketball and football teams often appear in Miami and in January 1996, BAC One-Eleven N119GA, carrying the titles and colours of the *Seattle Supersonics*, made an appearance. Well over 30 years old, the British-built aircraft appears to be in excellent external condition as it sits in the winter sunshine.

ABOVE: The Arrow Air personnel load and unload their DC-8s by fork-lift and N784AL was being prepared to accept a consignment of pallets via its side cargo door when photographed in April 1992.

OPPOSITE ABOVE: Miami-based freighter Arrow Air's facility is situated on the north side of the airport where their McDonnell Douglas DC-8s and Lockheed L1011s arrive and depart at regular intervals. All of this carrier's fleet have been converted from passenger configured aircraft to freighters. Photographed in January 1992, N798AL the DC-8 in the foreground, which has since been deleted from the Arrow fleet, is seen in the airline's original livery. Sister aircraft N345JW sports the newly applied scheme introduced in the early 1990s.

OPPOSITE BELOW: Arrow Air's first wide-body aircraft were delivered during 1996, Lockheed L1011s being chosen by the carrier. Three examples of the type are currently in service with 'Big A', all having previously flown in the colours of Gulf Air. In this January 1997 picture, two TriStars, N306GB and N307GB, are parked awaiting their next assignments.

BELOW: During 1993 the Colombian-based airline Avianca operated a Boeing 757 of the UK-based charter airline Ambassador on a short-term lease. The basic colours of the owner were retained with the titles of the leasing airline applied. G-BUDZ was one of two leased 757s in service with Avianca over a two-month period, terminating at the end of December 1993. Both aircraft returned to the United Kingdom to continue flying for Ambassador until the company ceased operations in November 1994.

OPPOSITE ABOVE: Airlift International was a Miami-based carrier, founded in 1945. The airline suspended operations in 1992 and at that time operated one McDonnell Douglas DC-8 as a freighter together with six Fairchild F27s configured to carry up to 40 passengers. A trio of F27s is parked on the Miami ramp, photographed in January 1992, only a few weeks prior to the airline's demise.

OPPOSITE BELOW: McDonnell Douglas DC-8 OB-1452, also illustrated on page 87 in the colours of Haiti Trans Air, was photographed in January 1992 whilst in the colours of the Peruvian airline Faucett. The vastness of the ramp area is apparent in this photograph.

ABOVE: In January 1997 a twice-weekly one-stop flight operated between Moscow and Miami. The aircraft used on this service were Airbus A310s, French-registered and leased to the Russian airline Aeroflot. The aircraft selected to operate this flight when photographed was F-OGYU which is seen about to touch down on runway 9L.

BELOW: Interesting observations can be made on the ramps assigned for parking and freight movements on Miami Airport's north side. This 1971 vintage McDonnell Douglas DC-8 is just one of more than twenty-four of the type in service with Air Transport International, a Little Rock, Arkansas-based freight airline. The first flight in revenue-earning service by N735PL was in the colours of Japan Air Lines as a passenger-carrying plane. Twenty-six years later in January 1997, the DC-8 was still at work.

ABOVE: When westerly winds prevail, runways 30 and 27L are used for most landing traffic, giving passengers seated in window seats superb views of Miami Beach and the downtown area whilst on final approach. America West Boeing 737 series 300 N327AW, photographed in December 1997, was above Miami Beach only a few minutes earlier and is now about to land on 'three zero'. The Boeing is showing off its new company colours.

ABOVE: Several airliners taken out of service by their owners arrive at Miami for conversion or maintenance prior to being repainted and put into service by new owners. In this shot taken in January 1993, Boeing 727 YV-856C is in the final stages of being prepared for the Venezuelan airline JD Valenciana. This company commenced flying in December 1992 as a passenger-carrying airline and the 727 illustrated was to join an existing Boeing 727. During the early part of 1993, several new destinations in North and South America were added to the carrier's routes, but due to problems encountered, the company ceased operations in November 1993.

OPPOSITE BELOW: Located north of runway 9L is the airport's newly constructed north side cargo and maintenance area. One of the residents of this 165,000 sq.ft. air cargo centre is Challenge Air Cargo. This carrier has been operating from its Miami base since 1985 and now provides scheduled cargo services between the US and Latin America with a fleet of Boeing 757s, McDonnell Douglas DC-10s, and at the time of writing, a Boeing 707 built in 1969.

ABOVE: Following an overnight flight, Polar Air Cargo's Boeing 747 N853FT was photographed early on a January 1997 morning as the tug slowly manoeuvred her into position on the ramp for unloading. Founded in 1993, Polar Air's fleet is entirely composed of Boeing 747s, all of which have been converted into freighters and equipped with side cargo doors. This particular aircraft now carries the name *Heather H. Hamilton*, having previously flown in passenger configuration for United Airlines and Pan American.

ABOVE AND OPPOSITE: A general view of the new cargo area shows aircraft at their stands in the process of being loaded and unloaded, whilst the camera zooms in to record Boeing 707 CP-1698 of Lloyd Aereo Boliviano being loaded with pallets via its side cargo door. This type of aircraft is still seen at regular intervals at Miami.

ABOVE: Formed in 1992, Fine Air is another of the many Miami-based cargo airlines which until operating the recently acquired L1011 TriStar, provided services with a fleet of leased McDonnell Douglas DC-8s. N44UA and N55FB joined the airline in its first few months of operations and are seen being prepared for flight in December 1993. In the background another DC-8 in the colours of the Colombian carrier Arca is being loaded with cargo.

OPPOSITE ABOVE: Ladeco Airlines is a Santiago-based international and domestic scheduled airline operating an extensive network within Chile. Its present fleet consists entirely of Boeing 737s configured for passenger use. In 1990, however, the airline provided freight services using a dedicated Boeing 707. This aircraft made regular flights to Miami from South America, and CC-CYA was photographed in January 1990 upon its arrival.

OPPOSITE BELOW: McDonnell Douglas DC-8 OB-1372 of Fuerza Aerea Del Peru is in combi-configuration and operates for the Peruvian Air Force, providing non-profit passenger and cargo flights to destinations not served by the country's civilian airlines. One such flight had been made by the aircraft photographed on the Miami ramp in January 1990.

OPPOSITE ABOVE AND BELOW: Prior to financial difficulties which necessitated the cessation of all operations in September 1998, Southern Air Transport, an Ohio-based specialist cargo transporter, had been operating services since its formation in 1947. Three types of aircraft were in service with the airline which will be best remembered for its fleet of Lockheed Hercules. In addition to this class of aircraft, Southern Air also included in their fleet examples of McDonnell Douglas DC-8s and converted Boeing 747s. The DC-8s were re-engined and classified series 73s. N871SJ, which was photographed in April 1992, remained in service with Southern Air until appearing in the colours of Emery Worldwide in 1994. The first of the carrier's 747s was originally constructed as a freighter without fuselage windows. Put into service in 1981, the Jumbo flew for 13 years in Japan Airways' colours before joining Southern Air in August 1994, when it received new colours and the registration N740SJ. When photographed in December 1994, the freighter was preparing to depart on an early afternoon flight.

BELOW: It is obviously essential to consult future flight programmes and park 747s correctly for untroubled exit when the time arrives for departure. These four Boeings were photographed in January 1998 whilst parked in line.

BELOW AND OPPOSITE: Facilities at the western end of the airfield carry out repairs to aircraft, some of which find new owners upon completion. Two McDonnell Douglas DC-8s, taken out of service by previous owners, are seen receiving the attention of engineers. As observed in these two shots taken in January 1998, not all servicing work is conducted inside hangars, and one engineer appears to be perfectly happy working on the wing in the southern Florida sun.

BELOW: Turning onto and about to depart Miami on runway 12 is Boeing 727 N745US, one of three recently-delivered aircraft to Laker, previously in service with USAir. This photograph, taken in December 1992, illustrates the final scheme applied to Laker aircraft following the completion of the repainting process shown in the initial stages in the shot on page 16.

OPPOSITE ABOVE: This Boeing 737 series 300 is about to commence its take-off on runway 12 in this photograph taken in December 1997. The airliner is displaying the new colour scheme of US Airways which was hitherto known as USAir.

OPPOSITE BELOW: McDonnell Douglas DC-9 XA-TCT of the Mexican airline Servicios Aerolineas Mexicanas was one of a fleet of two DC-9s operating within Mexico and North America at the time this photograph was taken in December 1994. This airline was founded in 1992 and operated until all flights were suspended in March 1995. The flight crew have received approval for take-off from Miami Tower and the jet is about to thunder down runway 12 to commence a return journey to Mexico.

OPPOSITE: Photographed in December 1995, a Tower Air Boeing 747 is about to make an early evening departure as the camera catches the Jumbo about to turn onto runway 9L. In the background can be seen Miami Tower from which all major points of the airfield can be observed.

ABOVE: The majority of easterly bound departing traffic for Central and South America normally elect to use runway 12, although of course there are exceptions. In December 1997, Air Aruba McDonnell Douglas MD-88 N11FQ keeps to this practice as it begins to line up for departure on its non-stop 2½-hour flight to Aruba.

ABOVE: Challenge Air Cargo Boeing 757 N571CA has selected runway 27L for landing, the runway chosen by the majority of freighters coming in from the east. After coming to a halt, the 757 will taxi to the CAC base situated in the newly constructed north-side cargo area. Challenge operate three Boeing 757s, all of which are constructed as cargo-carrying aircraft.

BELOW: Enthusiasts and photographers can observe the action at several points around the airport perimeter. South of the start of runway 9L one is able to view both landings and take-offs on that runway, together with flights using runway 12. As a general rule, runways 9L and 12 are used for landing traffic originating in the north, whilst the same two runways also accommodate departing traffic. This is of course only applicable when winds are easterly.

OPPOSITE ABOVE: About to touch down on runway 30 is an Airbus A320 making one of its first appearances in Miami in the recently applied colours of Grupo Taca, a scheme which will eventually be carried on all aircraft operated by Aviateca, Lacsa, Nica and Taca Airlines.

OPPOSITE BELOW: Operating a now discontinued service is Boeing 737 series 300 N304AL of the Kansas-based carrier Vanguard Airlines. This domestic carrier had a fleet of 737s and at the time this picture was taken, in January 1997, two of the series 300 models were included in the fleet. The latter models have since been replaced by additional series 200 Boeing 737s and the Miami service withdrawn. Runway 12 is again being used for take-off.

BELOW: Although Sun Country McDonnell Douglas DC-10 N571SC was destined for a North American city, runway 12 was being used when the airliner was photographed in January 1997. The aircraft's nose wheel is almost in normal position and the flight crew are awaiting clearance for departure. Sun Country is a Minneapolis-based charter passenger airline and include Boeing 727s in their fleet, supplementing DC-10s.

OPPOSITE ABOVE: Arriving on the mid-day flight from Mexico City in January 1998 is one of Mexicana's many Boeing 727s still in service with the carrier. XA-MEF carries the special 'Chivas' markings applied to celebrate the Guadalajara-based football team's success in a domestic cup competition. Mexicana are sponsors of the team.

OPPOSITE BELOW: Boeing 737 N121GU carries the colours of Aviateca, the airline of Guatemala. A daily flight operates from Guatemala City to Miami, the return flight departing from Florida in the early afternoon with all services being operated by 737s. This photograph, taken in January 1997, shows additional stickers applied to the fuselage of the Boeing to celebrate the signing of a peace treaty with guerrillas in Guatemala. When translated, 'Las Alas de La Paz' means 'The Wings of Peace'.

OPPOSITE ABOVE: Shorts 360 N261GA flies for Gulfstream International Airlines on routes to resorts in the Caribbean. Special markings have been applied to this aircraft and when photographed in January 1997, Grand Bahama Island main titles were to be seen.

OPPOSITE BELOW: N8041D is one of a small number of Dash 7s operated by Paradise Island Airlines, a Fort Lauderdale-based company. The airline originally had an affiliation with USAir but this was discontinued at the end of 1996, when aircraft were repainted in a new colour scheme incorporating a palm tree and bird against a yellow background.

ABOVE: Paradise Island Airlines changed its name to Prestige Airways at the end of 1995 and commenced services between Washington (Dulles) – Miami – St Thomas with Boeing 727 N74318 which is here seen about to turn onto runway 12 in December 1996. Operations continued for only a short period as the airline ceased flying in April 1997.

OPPOSITE: Cargo City is situated south of runways 12/30, where the majority of freight traffic passing through the airport is handled. With over two million tons of international cargo travelling through each year, Miami maintains its position as the number one airport in the United States for freight traffic.

ABOVE: The newly constructed cargo area seen from atop the control tower provides adequate space for several aircraft to be handled simultaneously. When this photograph was taken however, the facility was relatively quiet on account of the Christmas holiday.

OPPOSITE ABOVE: Boeing 707 CX-BPZ, carrying the colours of the Montevideo airline Aerosur, had completed push-back from the cargo terminal when photographed in January 1992, and was about to start its engines and taxi for take-off to Uruguay. This was the carrier's only aircraft at the time, being regularly put into service on the Miami route. The airline has since ceased operations.

OPPOSITE BELOW: Another regular visitor to the cargo terminal was the French airline UTA. This airline has also now disappeared from the scene following its merger with Air France in November 1992. Boeing 747 F-GBOX was one of two 747 freighters in the UTA fleet and was about to return to France when photographed in January 1991.

ABOVE: Aeromexpress is one of fourteen foreign scheduled all-cargo carriers operating to Miami. With a base in Mexico City, this airline's fleet consists of two Boeing 727s now flying in freight configuration, having previously flown as passenger airliners. N1279E had left the cargo ramp when photographed in January 1995 and was making its way to runway 12 for departure to Mexico.

ABOVE: Cargo City is host to many airlines from South and Central America and one regular visitor, photographed in May 1992, was the Montevideo-based airline Aerolineas Uruguayas who operated services to Miami with one Boeing 707. CX-BPL is in fact the same aircraft illustrated on page 56, seen visiting Cargo City four months earlier in the colours of Aerosur.

OPPOSITE ABOVE AND BELOW: Parcel and package carriers DHL and Federal Express also use the facilities provided by Cargo City. Seen in January 1992 are Boeing 727s flown by these two airlines. N721DH, in the colours of DHL, is being prepared for departure whilst sister ship N487FE is parked awaiting its next service.

ABOVE: Boeing 727 HP-1299PFC of Pacific International Airlines, photographed in December 1996, made regular appearances at that time being unloaded and loaded with freight at this remote ramp. This freight-carrying airline was formed in 1993 and from its base in Panama uses a fleet of two 727s.

ABOVE: Airliners withdrawn from service
often find themselves dumped at locations
around the airport awaiting a decision on
their future. In December 1993, a Boeing
727 of the Dominican airline Dominicana
and an L1011 TriStar belonging to Faucett
of Peru were photographed tightly parked
and out of service.

ABOVE: This L1011 TriStar of the Dominican carrier APA was making daily flights into Miami less than twelve months before this shot was taken. OB-1545 has unfortunately reached the end of its days and is one of the many airliners to be broken up at this Miami site.

ABOVE: Photographed two years earlier and featured on page 22 in much better external condition, Boeing 727 HC-BIB of SAN was later withdrawn from service and placed alongside another of the same type.YV-465C had been in service with the Venezuelan airline Zuliana prior to its withdrawal, and both airliners were in the process of being scrapped when photographed in January 1998. The SAN aircraft had seen twenty-six years of service, whilst the one flying for Zuliana before the closure of the airline in 1997 had been flying for thirty years,

RIGHT: The current Air Traffic Control Tower is the ninth to be constructed at the airfield and has been in use since 1985. The original Miami Tower was established on 1 May 1941, commencing operations with only three air traffic controllers – today there are 86.

Construction has already commenced on a new facility which will be positioned west of the current tower. Measuring 332 feet from the ground to the top of the radar dome, the observation deck will be 100 feet higher than that of the current tower and will provide visual control of all areas of the airport as the construction programme in hand enlarges the areas in use. This $16.9 million project is expected to be operational by October 2000.

ABOVE: With engines in reverse thrust, a
Boeing 767 of Avianca Colombia comes to
a halt on runway 30. The beautiful modern
skyline of downtown Miami five miles
distant is in the background, and to the
right of the picture can be seen the Miami
Orange Bowl Stadium.

ABOVE: This is the controller's view of operations from the top of Miami Tower. An Air Canada A320 Airbus has landed on runway 30 and turned around at one of the exits to make its way to the terminal buildings.

ABOVE: Captured by the camera seconds
after lift-off on runway 30, a Delta Air Lines
Lockheed L1011 takes to the sky.

ABOVE: Shown at gate number F7 in January 1997 is the newly delivered Airbus A320 N624AJ surrounded by fuel trucks, baggage carts and loaders. Delivered new to Air Jamaica only a matter of two or three weeks earlier, the twin-class airliner was immediately put into service on the short Kingston – Miami route, supplementing existing services operated by A310s.

OPPOSITE ABOVE: Airlines based in South and Central America park at gates situated on the north side of the terminal. Photographed in January 1998 was Boeing 727 YV-92C of the Venezuelan airline Servivensa, together with Lloyd Aereo Boliviano's Airbus A310 CP-2332, parked at adjacent gates.

OPPOSITE BELOW: Until the airline's demise in January 1991, the once mighty Eastern Airlines had their own gates at MIA, situated on concourse B. This picture shows a trio of Airbus A300s being prepared for flight together with a Boeing 727 parked at the end of the finger. This picture was taken in January 1991, and a few weeks later the airline passed into history.

OPPOSITE ABOVE: Airbus A300 OB 1596 was photographed in January 1995 being pushed back from the gate. It is an early appearance for the airliner, having only been delivered to the Peruvian airline Faucett in December 1994 and passing to APA in full colours on lease in January 1995. This airliner has appeared in Miami on several occasions whilst in service with Eastern Airlines and Pan American.

OPPOSITE BELOW: Making a departure from the eastern side of concourse B in April 1992 is Airbus Industrie A310 HC-BRP of Saeta. The current schedule shows a daily service in operation linking the cities of Quito and Guayaquil with Miami, now operated by Airbus A320 airliners.

ABOVE: The command 'gear up' appears to have been activated without delay as American Airlines Boeing 727 N712AA passes level with the control tower windows with the wheel compartment doors almost in closed position.

ABOVE: Prior to the cessation of services in 1993 and the subsequent recommencement of flights in early 1996, Ecuatoriana Airbus A310 HC-BRA was photographed entering the concourse F ramp, approaching the gate to discharge its passengers.

OPPOSITE ABOVE: Having just landed on runway 9R in January 1993, N501NG of the Nicaraguan airline Nica taxies along the front of concourse E, making its way to its allocated gate on the north side.

OPPOSITE BELOW: The airport's north-side concourse B receives an influx of traffic around noon with simultaneous arrivals from South and Central America. Boeing 727 HK-3738X of Aces Colombia is being refuelled for its return to Medellín, whilst Airbus A320 N482GX of Lacsa is being made ready for a departure to San Jose, Costa Rica.

ABOVE: Receiving the attention of the ground crew whilst parked on concourse F gate 18 is the Venezuelan airline Viasa's Boeing 727 YV-128C. It would appear that both freight and passengers will be carried on this flight. Photographed in early January 1997, this was to be one of the last appearances of the Viasa colours in Miami as the airline ceased operations two weeks after the picture was taken.

BELOW: A twice-weekly flight from the South African cities of Cape Town and Johannesburg arrives in Miami at 05.25 hours. After passengers have disembarked and arrival formalities have been concluded, the aircraft is towed to a remote parking area before being brought back to the gate in the early afternoon in readiness for a 17.00 hours departure. Boeing 747 series 400 ZS-SAY was operating this flight when photographed in January 1996 and is seen under the control of the tractor.

ABOVE: Photographed in January 1996, having dispensed with the services of the push tractor, Air South Boeing 737 N159PL slowly pulls away from its gate on concourse H, making its way via various taxiways to the departure runway. Air South commenced operations from its Atlanta base in 1993 with a fleet of 737 twin-jets, but ceased operations in September 1997.

LEFT: Metro-Dade Aviation Department provide a very important service to the airport with their fully equipped Fire Department. Situated mid-field, the personnel employed at this facility are permanently on stand-by to attend any emergency that may arise.

BELOW: The gates for passengers joining flights operated by Gulfstream International Airlines are via concourse F, and intending flyers board the aircraft on the ramp. Being prepared for flight in January 1998 are two Beechcraft 1900 nineteen-seat aircraft.

ABOVE: The commuter satellite is located away from the concourses and it is necessary for passengers to be transported to their aircraft. American Eagle is a subsidiary of American Airlines and operates commuter services out of Miami to destinations in Florida. N204NE is a Saab 340 thirty-four-seat commuter airliner and was photographed in January 1998 being prepared to board passengers.

OPPOSITE ABOVE: American International Airlines McDonnell Douglas DC-8 N805CK, photographed in January 1998, is only a few hundred feet away from touching down on runway 27L. This freighter is seen in an all-white scheme and is part of the Kalitta fleet still in the original series 51 classification.

OPPOSITE BELOW: Lining up for an immediate departure on runway 9R in December 1994 is McDonnell Douglas DC-10 OH-LHA with World titles and tail logo and the colours of the North American airline Express One. The DC-10 is in the fleet of Finnair and had been on lease to Express One before being put into service on World flights.

ABOVE: Arriving mid-afternoon at its Florida destination after completing a non-stop flight of almost 5,000 miles, is Spain's national flag carrier Iberia's Boeing 747 EC-GAG. This daily flight connects in Miami with flights to and from Guatemala, Nicaragua, Panama and Costa Rica – all operated by Iberia's Central America-based McDonnell Douglas DC-9s.

OPPOSITE ABOVE: Amerijet International is one of Florida's freight airlines with bases in Fort Lauderdale and Miami. It operates a fleet of 14 Boeing 727s. The majority of destinations served by the airline are situated within the Caribbean and Mexico. On final approach to runway 30 in January 1998 is N797AJ, at that time the latest aircraft to join the fleet.

OPPOSITE BELOW: Miami is the ideal location to log and photograph airliners from South and Central America, as it is possible that representatives from many of those countries àre at the airport on most days of the week. In January 1992, Douglas DC-7 HI-599CT was photographed discharging its cargo for Customs examination. Built in 1957, this Douglas classic later flew for the Dominican Republic airline Aerochago, joining the carrier in the summer of 1991.

ABOVE: Digex Aero Cargo is a Brazilian company which until recently provided services with their sole aircraft – a Boeing 727. At the end of 1997, a McDonnell Douglas DC-8 was being prepared for a five-year lease to the company and PP-MDF was in the final stages of preparation prior to being handed over to the airline when it was photographed in January 1998.

OPPOSITE ABOVE: BWIA International, the airline of the Caribbean with a base in Trinidad, was the first airline in the area to put the new Airbus A321 into service, leasing two of the type in the summer of 1996 and operating them on the Port of Spain – Miami and Port of Spain – New York routes. 9Y-BWB was the second A321

OPPOSITE BELOW: Trinity Air Bahamas was a short-lived airline founded in 1992 and based in Nassau. Their fleet consisted of two McDonnell Douglas DC-9s which made frequent visits to MIA on passenger services between the mainland and

to be delivered on lease to BWIA and was photographed in January 1997 on approach to runway 30, completing its flight from Port of Spain. The Airbuses remained in the fleet for only a short time and were returned to the leasing company for onward lease to the Turkish airline Air Alfa in the spring of 1997.

the Caribbean Islands. N1290L was photographed in December 1993 about to touch down on runway 9L. Trinity Air continued operations for a further five months after this shot was taken.

OPPOSITE ABOVE: VASP operate a McDonnell Douglas MD-11 on their Rio de Janeiro to Miami service. PP-SPE is one of eight of the type currently in VASP colours and was photographed in December 1996 on the completion of its journey from Brazil.

OPPOSITE BELOW: To the east of the PMS hangar is the Commodore facility where repairs and conversions are performed. Boeing 737 series 200 XA-TCQ had just emerged from the hangar for an engine run-up and tests when photographed in

ABOVE: Continuing further east and running parallel to NW36 Street are more hangars under the control of other companies providing services to airlines. McDonnell Douglas DC-10 HC-BKO is seen receiving attention and now carries the new colours of Ecuatoriana, recently applied prior to the re-commencement of services by the Quito, Ecuador-based

December 1992, prior to being handed over to the Mexican airline Saro. This Monterrey-based carrier continued to provide passenger services until all flights were suspended in March 1995.

carrier in early 1996. This airline temporarily suspended operations in September 1993 and at that time the aircraft illustrated was flying in the flamboyant colours by which Ecuatoriana were known. Upon the return to service, the airline became a subsidiary of the Brazilian carrier VASP and the aircraft was re-registered to become PP-SFB.

BELOW: Photographed in January 1997, prior to its visit to the maintenance hangar later that year and also illustrated on page 20, Staf Cargo McDonnell Douglas DC-10 XA-TDC is seen in service operating a cargo flight from South America. The crew have elected to land on runway 30, making it more convenient to taxi to a stand used by the carrier on the north side of the airport. Staf Cargo is an Argentinian airline based in Buenos Aires and this DC-10 joined the airline in May 1996.

ABOVE: The north-east corner of the airport contains hangars and ramp areas where aircraft are parked and maintained. McDonnell Douglas DC-8 OB-1452 carries Haiti Trans Air titles and colours, applied whilst leased during the period February 1992 to March 1993. Photographed in January 1993, the airliner is seen in its final hours, as it was withdrawn from service in March of that year.

LEFT: The same ramp area was accommodating sister aircraft N43UA at the time, a 1964-built machine originally flying as a passenger-carrying airliner for United Air Lines. Sitra Cargo is part of the Aero Peru system and when photographed this DC-8 was the only pure freighter in the Aero Peru fleet. N43UA came to grief in April 1995 when it crashed upon landing at Guatemala City.

BELOW: In late afternoon December sunshine, Lufthansa Boeing 747 D-ABZD taxies to the holding point on runway 9L to prepare for departure to Frankfurt. Following its arrival, the Jumbo has spent almost two hours at the gate being made ready for flight, and its overnight journey will mean arrival at the German city before 06.00 hours local time.

OPPOSITE ABOVE: Flights between the United Kingdom and Florida by Laker Airways were again operating during 1997 with scheduled services between London's Gatwick Airport and Miami. These flights were withdrawn shortly after this photograph of McDonnell Douglas DC-10 N831LA coming in to land on runway 12 was taken in January 1998.

OPPOSITE BELOW: Boeing 737 N67AF has found a parking slot on the ramp adjacent to NW57 Avenue. Carrying the titles and colours of Haiti Trans Air, this twin-jet was one of the first 737s to appear, emerging from the Boeing plant in February 1969. When photographed in December 1990, N67AF was on a three-month lease to the carrier. Although originally delivered to United Air Lines when new, the registration N67AF was applied in 1980 when the aircraft was bought by Air Florida and the airliner has since retained this identification.

ABOVE: Virgin Atlantic operate a daily service to Miami from London Heathrow, their Boeing 747 touching down mid-afternoon. Photographed in December 1996, G-VOYG had been seen in the sky ten minutes before as it flew downwind over North Miami before making a long left turn to line up on the glidepath for runway 9L.

ABOVE: Air Europa is an international charter airline based in Palma de Mallorca. Its present fleet is made up of almost thirty aircraft, predominately Boeing 737s but also including Boeing 757s and 767s which are put into service on the carrier's longer routes. The airline operates a seasonal service to Florida, using 767s on these flights. EC-GHM, which bears the name *Palma de Mallorca*, was photographed about to touch down on runway 12 in December 1996. It is configured all economy class with seating for 238 passengers.

ABOVE: In a pure white Faucett livery, Lockheed L1011 OB-1659 is seen arriving on 'three zero' in December 1996. Based in Lima, Peru, Faucett operated regular services into Miami until their wide-body airliners were withdrawn from the fleet. The airline continued to provide services to destinations within South America with Boeing 727s and 737s until finally ceasing flights in November 1997.

BELOW: The scene at the PMS facility is constantly changing as aircraft depart and new ones arrive for attention. In this April 1992 photograph, Boeing 727 N915TS now carries the livery of USAir after being in service with Trump Shuttle, a New York-based airline founded by Donald Trump which was taken over by USAir.

ABOVE: LWA – Liberia World Airlines – was founded in 1974 with a European base in the Belgium town of Ostende. When photographed in April 1992, McDonnell Douglas DC-8 EL-AJQ was one of four aircraft in service. There was also another DC-8 plus two Boeing 707s. This DC-8 still flies for the airline but the Boeing airliners have since been withdrawn.

OPPOSITE ABOVE: United Parcel Service (UPS) is one of North America's major package carriers, operating a fleet of more than 200 aircraft. Their colours are

OPPOSITE BELOW: Parking facilities are available for private and executive aircraft at the General Aviation facility. Arriving at this location in January 1988 was Skyway Enterprises Shorts 330 N2629Y, now configured as a freighter. This airline is

regularly to be seen in Miami and photographed arriving on a January 1998 afternoon is Boeing 727 N947UP.

based in Kissimee, Florida. As Miami International Airport continues to grow, the general aviation and related activities situated at other conveniently located airports will provide a significant role as they alleviate traffic at MIA.

ABOVE: The late afternoon sunshine is a bonus for the photographer and was put to full advantage to record the landing of Western Pacific's Boeing 737 series 300 N947WP in January 1997. This Colorado Springs-based airline, famous for its flying logos and advertising on the sides of its airliners, operated a daily flight from Colorado Springs to Miami for a short period. These flights were later to be discontinued, and the airline ceased operations completely in February 1998.

BELOW: Cargo service between the Israeli capital Tel Aviv and Miami is operated by that country's national airline El Al. When photographed in January 1997, Boeing 747 4X-AXF was making a late afternoon approach to runway 27L, followed by unloading and re-loading at Cargo City.

ABOVE: A small number of airlines still operate propeller-driven aircraft on freight services, and in January 1992 the Honduras-based airline Sahsa provided services to Miami with their only example of a Lockheed Electra, HR-SHN. This is a 1959-built machine and has flown for Sahsa since 1984.

OPPOSITE ABOVE: With runway 30 only a few seconds away, Lockheed L1011 TriStar OB-1455 of the Peruvian airline Faucett safely brings its passengers to earth in

OPPOSITE BELOW: Sahsa also provide passenger services from Honduras to Miami, and one of these flights was photographed in January 1992. Boeing 737 N3160M is seen about to touch down on runway 30. The south side of the

January 1992. At that time the airline was sharing capacity with Aero Peru on the Lima – Miami route, which accounted for the additional Aero Peru titles.

terminal buildings is visible in the background where a Tower Air Boeing 747 and a United airliner are parked at their gates. Sahsa suspended all operations in January 1994.

ABOVE: Missouri-based North American freight carrier American International Airways was originally known as 'Kalitta', named after its founder Connie Kalitta. With a large fleet of over 40 McDonnell Douglas DC-8s, Lockheed L1011s and Boeing 747s, the airline's colours are regularly observed at Miami. Before 1994 this airline was totally committed to the transportation of freight, but has now added passenger-configured airliners to its fleet. Photographed whilst parked on the north-western ramp area in December 1995, Lockheed L1011 N103CK was originally a passenger airliner flying in the colours of British Airways and British Airtours, before being converted to a freighter.

ABOVE: A ramp to the west of the PMS facility is used to park aircraft before and after maintenance. In this instance, McDonnell Douglas DC-9 N8938E was brought here after being repainted and having the titles Zenith Air applied.

Originally an Eastern Airlines aircraft, this series 31 model, photographed in December 1992, was leased to the Nigerian airline and subsequently registered 5N-GIN. It was to become a very short leasing period as Zenith Air suspended operations in July 1993 and the aircraft returned to the States to become N8938E again, finding further service in the colours of Northwest Airlines.

ABOVE: The sun has just about set as a Boeing 707 in the colours of the Colombian airline Tampa comes in to land. At the time of writing, Tampa still operate three of these classic airliners together with two McDonnell Douglas DC-8 series 71s. The airline operate into and out of Miami on a regular basis and their colours can be seen on most days.

BELOW: Another South American airline to visit Miami is Aeca, a small Ecuadorian carrier based in Guayaquil. At the time of writing, the airline's cargo services are operated by two Boeing 707s but an arriving freight service, when photographed in January 1995, was operated by Boeing 727 HC-BRF.

ABOVE: To provide extra capacity on services from Miami to the Bahamas through the Christmas/New Year 1992/3 period, Bahamasair leased Airbus Industrie A320 G-OOAC from the United Kingdom airline Air 2000 for two months. The airliner operated in the basic colours of its owner during this period but with additional Bahamasair titles. Brakes had just been released and the twin-jet was photographed at the start of its take-off roll.

OPPOSITE ABOVE: Millon Air, formed in 1983 as a Miami-based cargo-carrying airline was regularly seen on the Miami ramps, their services being operated by a small fleet of McDonnell Douglas DC-8s and Boeing 707s. During the latter part of 1996, the airline added a Lockheed L1011 to the fleet upon the conversion to a freighter of an LTU German airline

OPPOSITE BELOW: Until its merger with the new Pan American, Carnival Air Lines were a Fort Lauderdale-based charter and scheduled carrier. To allow for extra capacity during the Christmas holiday period, Carnival also found it necessary to lease additional airliners to accommodate the extra passengers booked on their

passenger aircraft. The TriStar received the Millon Air colours but never flew in revenue-earning service for its new owners, spending most of its time on the company ramp. The airline ceased operations at the beginning of 1998 and the L1011 was repainted and now flies for another Miami-based cargo airline – Fine Air.

flights. Boeing 737 series 400 TC-AFM was flown over the Atlantic from Turkey and operated flights for the Floridian airline in the colours of the Turkish airline Pegasus and with additional Carnival stickers. The Boeing had just lined up and was about to take off on runway 27L when photographed in December 1995.

OPPOSITE ABOVE: An Airbus A320 in the Saeta Airlines fleet was photographed in December 1995 whilst bearing the additional title Air Ecuador. The aircraft is

OPPOSITE BELOW: Boeing 737-400 N401KW was a member of the Carnival fleet and was photographed in December 1994 with the additional fuselage title 'Fly Cruise', applied for the carrier's winter programme.

about to land on runway 30 after completing a flight from Guayaquil, a service shared by three other carriers. They all return to South America within 40 minutes of each other.

ABOVE: There are no specific times to expect the arrival of cargo-carrying aircraft in Miami. Such is the involvement in freight that an aircraft devoted purely to cargo transportation can be expected at any time of the day. An afternoon arrival in January 1996 of Atlas Air Boeing 747 N509MC attracted the interest of the photographer as it approached runway 27L.

ABOVE: Photographed in January 1995
whilst still in flying condition, Lockheed
L1011 OB-1545 makes a turn on to runway
27L whilst operating a scheduled service
to Santo Domingo. Leased from the
Peruvian airline Faucett, the full colours of
APA have been applied to the airliner. The
TriStar saw a further two years in service
before being withdrawn and subsequently
scrapped, and is illustrated on page 62 in
the first stages of dismantlement.

BELOW: The Venezuelan airline Viasa used to be a regular visitor to MIA, operating services to Caracas until the company ceased operations. The flights were performed by McDonnell Douglas DC-10s and the afternoon departure photographed in January 1995 was being operated by YV-137C, ready to go on runway 27L.

OPPOSITE ABOVE: Tower Air's main operations are international and charter passenger services and fourteen of their Boeing 747s are configured all-economy class with 480 seats. However, two 747s are pure freighters and operate cargo services to the Far East and destinations in the Pacific. Boeing 747 N493GX, photographed in January 1995 on finals to runway 27L, was bought by Tower Air a few weeks earlier and still carries the registration of a leasing company. It was re-registered one month after being photographed and now carries its present registration N613FF.

OPPOSITE BELOW: Boeing 747 N608FF is passenger-configured and carries the full colours of Tower Air. It was photographed in January 1998 after landing on runway 30. The airliner has exited the active runway, turned around and is slowly proceeding to a gate for passenger disembarkation.

ABOVE: Shortly after the arrival of Tower Air Cargo, another freighter was seen on approach to 27L. The fleet of Millon Air mainly consisted of Boeing 707s until the airline ceased operations in October 1996. In this picture the classic Boeing product, N751MA, is only a few feet from putting all ten wheels on the ground.

ABOVE: Another Miami day comes to a close, the sun has disappeared beyond the horizon but activity at the airport continues. An American Airlines MD-11 lines up for a landing on runway 9L whilst in the distance another inbound service can be seen about to lower landing gear to land on 9R.